Serge SIKA Ngonda

# The Dewaz Method

**Serge SIKA Ngonda**

# The Dewaz Method

**For the preparation, execution, monitoring and evaluation of state and company budgets**

**ScienciaScripts**

**Imprint**

Any brand names and product names mentioned in this book are subject to trademark, brand or patent protection and are trademarks or registered trademarks of their respective holders. The use of brand names, product names, common names, trade names, product descriptions etc. even without a particular marking in this work is in no way to be construed to mean that such names may be regarded as unrestricted in respect of trademark and brand protection legislation and could thus be used by anyone.

Cover image: www.ingimage.com

This book is a translation from the original published under ISBN 978-620-6-69364-2.

Publisher:
Sciencia Scripts
is a trademark of
Dodo Books Indian Ocean Ltd. and OmniScriptum S.R.L publishing group

120 High Road, East Finchley, London, N2 9ED, United Kingdom
Str. Armeneasca 28/1, office 1, Chisinau MD-2012, Republic of Moldova, Europe
Printed at: see last page
**ISBN: 978-620-7-27693-6**

Contents

Serge SIKA began his career as a researcher in budgeting techniques when, in 1995, he was involved in the management of a school where he worked as a standing teacher. Suddenly, he realised that forecasting financial management was a real problem due to the lack of appropriate management tools.

He therefore embarked on a highly complex field of research in order to find the necessary means for effective management. This research led to the development of a budgeting method which had been called the "School Budget by Tables" and which, after successive improvements, came to be known as the "Dewaz Method", deemed appropriate for school management.

The Dewaz Method has subsequently been reformed and extended, so that it can be adapted to all sectors of activity, both public and private, and is no longer just a management tool for schools.

Serge SIKA's current aim is to use the results of his research to turn budgeting into a scientific discipline in its own right. This is the raison d'etre of the collection ". Les pratiques budgetaires".

# FOREWORD

*This handbook is a combined tool for government and corporate budget management, with the aim of providing the basic elements for effective and efficient budget management.*

*The story began when American practitioners, in the wake of the 1929 crisis which had hit their country hard, devised a budgeting method which was exhibited at the same time in several other Western countries, but it was only after the Second World War that it was widely accepted. This method of budgeting proved to be very effective, but remained the preserve of practitioners, because, as Meyer writes, there was no general theory to provide guidelines for drawing up and using budgets.[1]*

*A number of researchers in many countries, notably Jean Meyer in France, had undertaken work to clarify the fundamental concepts and objectives of budget management.*

*It is in this sense that the scientific investigations, namely the detailed study of budgetary management, which were undertaken to provide the knowledge necessary to put an end to systematic financial extravagance, were the first steps towards the development of what is now known as the Dewaz Method, a scientific approach based on the use of supplementary tables to draw up, implement and evaluate the budgets of states and companies, both public and private.*

*The Dewaz Method enables good governance insofar as it acts as a management tool that takes into account all the essential functions of a structure, then, as a budgetary method, it is defined as an ideal basis for effective and efficient management of States and companies of all kinds with a view to providing objective support, on the one hand, company managers to strengthen good governance, and on the other, the public administration to set up a practical and effective system for monitoring the management of public and private companies.*

*The combination of the Dewaz method with budget algebra solves the problem of flexibility and precision described by Professor Paul Seka Seka, because for a long time revenue evaluation methods were recommended to avoid the risk of arbitrariness in revenue evaluation. But today, all these methods are set to be abandoned in favour of methods that are both precise and flexible.[2]*

*I would like to express my gratitude to my dear wife Lydie SIKA for her moral and material contribution to the production of this book.*

*I would like to thank Mademoiselle Belcance NZUZI for the time she devoted to*

---

[1] J. MEYER, Gestion budgetaire, Paris, 1979, p 2
[2] SEKA SEKA Paul, Cours des Finances Publiques, Abidjan, 2012, p 10

*writing this book.*
*I would like to express my gratitude in advance to all those who are willing to send me their comments and suggestions for improving this work, which I recognise is not perfect.*

*Serge SIKA Ngonda*

Today, the study of the budget is presented as a synthesis of theoretical and practical knowledge relating to the concrete problems posed by the functioning and organisation of States and public and private companies.

The field of investigation of companies has been considerably modified and extended, and we have had to take account of this extension to analyse the operation of States and companies, in a purely budgetary context, without forgetting that the company budget is currently a less exploited field, insofar as research most often revolves around the State budget.

A budgeting method is therefore needed to clarify the principles for drawing up and using both state and company budgets. The method discussed in this book is the Dewaz Method, which recommends estimating revenue on the basis of the number and monetary value of budgetary products, which are the sources of revenue. This makes the Dewaz Method not only mathematical, but also compatible with both state and company budgets.

The book is organised into six chapters, each of which is developed in turn. The first chapter gives an overview of the Dewaz Method.

Chapters two and three describe the concepts of products and activities respectively.

Chapter Four gives a detailed view of the forecast amount which forms the basis of the budget forecasts.

Chapter Five develops the agricultural budget, i.e. the budgetary management of natural products.

Chapter Six, the last chapter of the book, is essentially devoted to the three applications of the Dewaz Method: budgeting, the budget procedure and the Integrated Budget System (IBS).

# Chapter I

# GENERAL INFORMATION ON THE DEWAZ METHOD

## I.2 What is the Dewaz Method?

The Dewaz Method is a budgeting method. It consists of :

1)  To present the financial information of a public or private organisation in supplementary tables, and to process them in such a way as to arrive at a table combining the revenue to be generated and the expenditure to be committed, the latter table being the best expression of the organisation's budget (worksheets);

2)  Record the revenue forecast in the budget, then allocate it and finally display the expenditure according to the status of each activity in the budget;

3)  Evaluate the budget on the basis of the combination tables.

The Dewaz Method is applied using complementary tables and in three phases:

> Budget preparation ;

> Budget execution ;

> Budget assessment.

Each phase has its own group of specific displayboards. The displayboards for the first phase are called design displayboards; those for the second phase are management displayboards, and the third group comprises mosaic displayboards.

| Design tables | | Management tables | | Mosaic paintings |
|---|---|---|---|---|

1. Management fund

2. Product directory

3. Headcount survey

4. Concordant subjects

5. Cost estimate 5. Activity grant

6. Evaluating production costs

7. Product breakdown

8. Centralising revenues

9. Description of expenditure

10. Summary

1. Financial

2. Perception report

3. Periodic revenue

4. Accumulation register

1. Backlog sheet

2. Summary stock exchange

3. Capitalist

A. Budget preparation

Budget preparation involves determining in advance the revenue and expenditure to be generated when no revenue has yet been generated and no expenditure has yet been incurred.

The idea is not to produce a budget based on vaguely estimated data, but to work with data that has been carefully calculated and rigorously checked.

The aim of forecasting," writes Fahey, "is to develop plausible operations in terms of the scale, direction, speed and intensity of change.[3]

According to Lesourne, it is possible to characterise each decision by the discounted income it generates and to choose the one for which the discounted income is maximum. It should be noted that, if information is perfect, this decision is also the one that maximises the value of the firm on the market, since this is nothing other than the present value of the firm's future profits.[3][4][5]

Drawing up a budget means listing, identifying and classifying expenditure and income, then making adjustments to achieve a balanced budget or the desired margin.

The length of time it takes to draw up a budget depends on the amount of financial information available to the company. For example, it may take just one day to prepare a budget for a small company, whereas it may take several months to prepare a budget for a large company.

There is one mistake we must not make," says Lesourne, "and that is to study an item of equipment without considering its replacement. So, he continues, each present decision is associated with a series of random future situations, the word random being taken in the sense of the theory of probabilities. More precisely, the present value of the future profits generated by a decision is a random variable whose probability distribution is assumed to be known.[5]

Total sales over a given period generally consist of a series of transactions with different margins covering more or less proportional fractions of operating costs. Careful analysis is always required to ensure that the average profit margin is sufficient.

**The number one rule for budget success:**

Sales targets need to be precisely defined. Ideally, these should be set for each market and business sector, as well as for each product line and customer segment.

B. Budget execution

Budget execution consists of implementing revenue and expenditure in accordance with the budget forecasts drawn up in the first phase.

The company should refer to its budget regularly during the financial year, if possible on a monthly basis. Any change in one of the items in the table may have a significant impact.

The estimated budget is provisional. It will therefore be subject to change as additional information becomes available to the company during the financial

---


[3] L. FAHEY, les parametres essentiels de la gestion strategiques, Paris, 1997, p 297
[4] L. LESOURNE, Technique economique et gestion industrielle, Paris, 1971, p 35
[5] L. LESOURNE, Technique economique et gestion industrielle, Paris, 1971, p 36

year:

- New supplies to buy
- Change of supplier
- Additional tax payable
- New customers to equip
- Market trends (upwards or downwards)
- Improvement or deterioration in the economic situation
- Prices and quantity of labour available
- Prices and levels of raw materials, etc.

**Regie numero deux :**

The company's performance should be compared regularly (every month or every three months) with the forecasts, and the forecasts should be modified if they prove to be too far off the mark.

C. Budget assessment

Budget evaluation consists of comparing actual and forecast figures in order to identify any discrepancies. This involves reconciling the design tables with the management tables to produce mosaic tables for evaluation purposes.

Budgetary control is a powerful investigative tool, because it provides a critical comparison between what should have happened and what did happen, between what was planned and what was actually achieved.[6]

It is in this sense that the Dewaz Method provides for budget evaluation by reconciling the design tables kept during budget preparation with the management tables used during budget execution. The exercise is straightforward and, at the end of the budgetary period, enables us not only to identify the differences between actual and forecast expenditure, but also to determine the budget implementation rate, which sets the targets for the next budget.

D. The budget period

The budget is always linked to a period of budgetary management, which is preceded by forecasting and completed by re-evaluation.

The generally accepted period is the annual period, because the accounts are closed annually and thus provide the elements for control.[7] But this period, whose merit is simplicity, does not always meet the requirements of a budgetary period. It will often be necessary to extend or deduct it.

It is desirable for companies to adopt shorter budget periods so that if an important event occurs during the budget period which alters the forecasts, there will be no hesitation in stopping the current period and substituting a new one.

---

[6] P. LOEB, Le budget de l'entreprise, Paris, 1956, p 76
[7] P. LOEB, Le budget de l'entreprise, Paris, 1956, p 78

This is how LOEB developed the theory that "there is no lower limit to the budget period, it must be modelled on the corresponding circumstances and measures".[8] If sales are seasonal, the budget must also be seasonal.

## I.3 Formalism of the Dewaz Method

A.  Origin

The difficulties of the budgetary principles studied in Public Finance in presenting a practical method for managing company budgets led to the search for a high-performance tool, and the creation of the Dewaz Method with its complementary tables (the practice of budget worksheets).

This is a management process that implements the properties of array succession, from design arrays through management arrays to mosaics.

A table is therefore a specific step in budget management.

B.  Features

In order to meet its stated aim of facilitating budget management in public and private companies, the Dewaz Method is essentially compatible with the principles of modularity. The budget worksheets are produced in three phases:

* Elaboration,
* Execution,
* Assessment.

Each phase has its own group of displayboards. The displayboards for the first phase are called design displayboards; those for the second phase are management displayboards, and the third group of displayboards comprises mosaic displayboards.

C.  Components

The budget worksheets include tables divided into three groups:

* Design tables ;
* Management charts ;
* Mosaic paintings.

| Design tables | Management tables |
|---|---|
| 1.  The management fund | 1.  Pecuniary |
| 2.  Product directory | 2.  The perception report |
| 3.  The workforce survey | 3.  The periodical |
| 4.  The concordant of subjects | 4.  The accumulation register |
| 5.  Costing | 5.  The activity exchange |

---

[8] P. LOEB, Le budget de l'entreprise, Paris, 1956, p 78

6.  Evaluating production costs
7.  Product breakdown
8.  Centralising revenue
9.  Description of expenditure
10. Summary

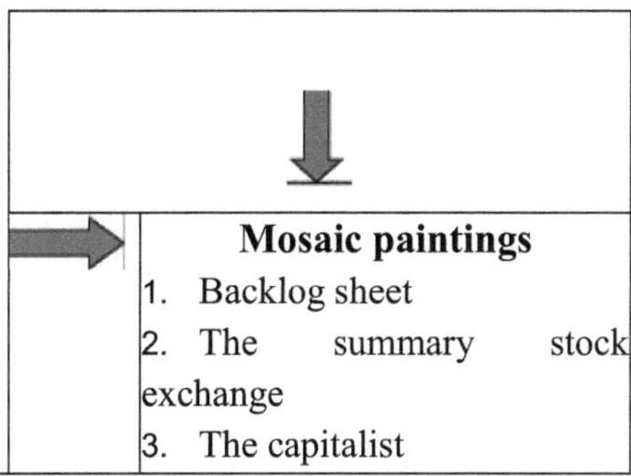



The tables in the Dewaz Method are complementary, but so are the groups of tables that make up the phases of the method, so the phases of the method are complementary from first to last.

The first phase closes with the handover to the second phase, whose material is found in the first phase. The second phase implements the first phase by giving concrete form to what was planned.

The third phase combines the first two phases to bring out the material required for the decision to be taken.

If the first phase precedes the second and gives it matter, the second precedes the third whose matter comes from both the first and the second.

So the second phase results from the first, but the third results from both the first and the second.

D. Basic structure

The worksheets budget is produced in three phases which form a whole inseparable.

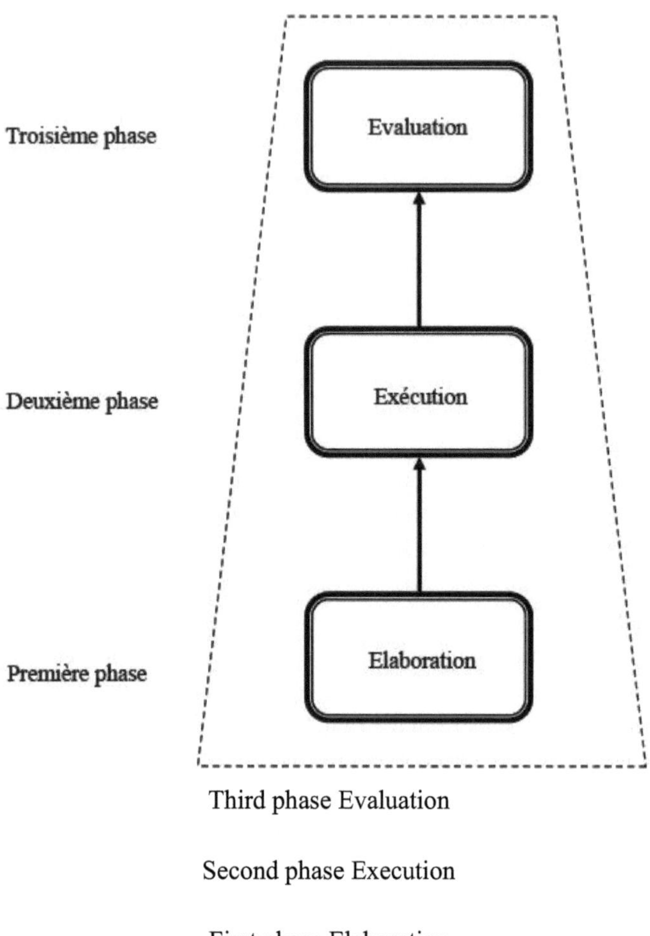



Third phase Evaluation

Second phase Execution

First phase Elaboration

The first phase prepares the second, and the first two prepare the third. As a result, the second phase cannot be carried out without the first, and the third phase cannot be carried out without the first two.

Is it possible to implement a budget that has not been drawn up in advance? Or assess a budget that has not been drawn up or implemented?

E. Phases in the budget cycle

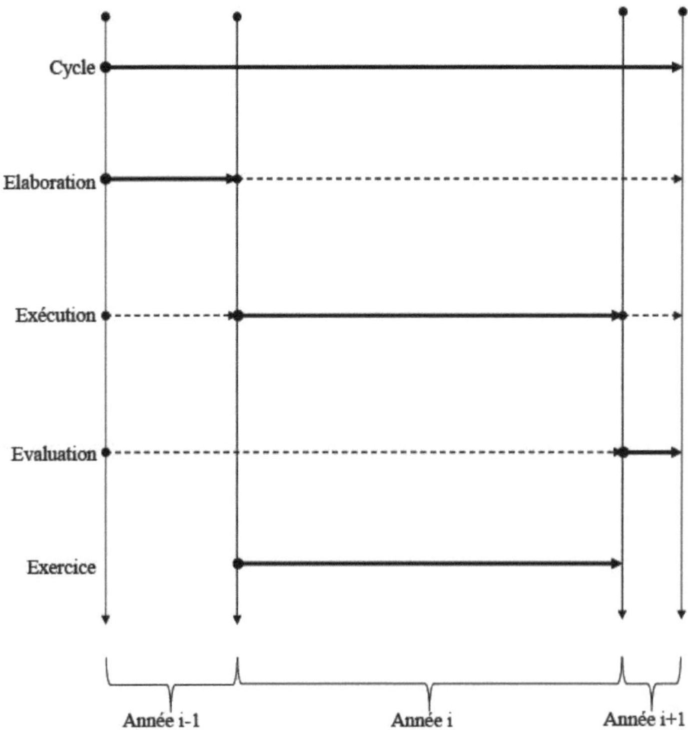



For an annual budget, the periodicity is one year, but its cycle extends over three successive years: the year of the budget and the preceding and following years. Only the execution takes place during the budget year, as the preparation takes place during the previous year and the evaluation during the following year.

F. Advantages of the Dewaz Method

Budget worksheets are a powerful method of presenting a company's financial information in a harmonious sequence, from the presentation of revenue sources to the determination of variances, using complementary tables.

The Dewaz Method is based on a highly formalised approach: a distinction is made between the three phases of the method: budget preparation, execution and re-evaluation, each of which has specific tables to be kept. As the 3 phases are complementary, the tables for each of these phases are also complementary. There is therefore a separation between the budget preparation, execution and evaluation functions.

The Dewaz Method is based on the study and manipulation of budgetary products and budgetary activities, with a view to defining the most effective operating method for carrying out specific budgetary management tasks, leading to the drawing up of an optimal transcription plan based on a succession of tables to be kept using precise rules and adapted formulas.

The Dewaz Method is based on a scientific approach to organising work in a formalised and standardised way, enabling the company budget to be drawn up, implemented and evaluated, with the possibility of identifying the variances between forecast and actual at the end of the financial year.

The Dewaz Method defines the possibility of achieving a potential budget surplus by studying and controlling the social factors that are at the root of the seasonal fluctuations that lead to budget imbalances, as well as the negative variances between actuals and forecasts, in the knowledge that it is possible not only to control them, but also to eliminate them.

With its complementary tables divided into three phases, the Dewaz Method makes management easier, simply by keeping the tables prepared using adapted formulas and simple, practical principles in a harmonious sequence comprising, on the one hand, the operations to be carried out and, on the other, the specialists whose respective tasks are directly linked to the budgetary operations.

The Dewaz Method is not a cold, rigid reality: it adapts to all kinds of businesses, both public and private, and to all of life's activities, from the simplest individual acts to the complex work of large companies.

## I.4 Principles of the Dewaz Method

A.  Principle of modularity

*Budget preparation, management, monitoring and the determination of variances must be carried out with precision product by product, activity by activity and consumer by consumer.*

The aim of modularity is to facilitate the tasks involved in drafting, steering, monitoring and identifying variances. The result is transparency in budget management, from drafting to re-evaluation.

Modularity advocates product-by-product, activity-by-activity and consumer-by-consumer management before overall management. Single management prepares the way for overall management.

It's easier to manage a single product, activity or consumer than to manage them all at once.

B.  Principle of monthly payment

*A good budget must be drawn up, implemented and evaluated on a month-by-month basis.* This is the only way not only to avoid being surprised by seasonal variations in the company's activities, but also to ensure a balance between the company's income and activities throughout the financial year.

The principles of modularity and monthly payment apply to all three phases of the budget: preparation, execution and evaluation.

A distinction must be made, however, because there is predictive modularity, active modularity and critical modularity, on the one hand, and predictive monthlyity, active monthlyity and critical monthlyity, on the other.

C.  Principle of realism

Budget realism is the expression of conformity with reality in the preparation and execution of the budget.

1.  Realistic forecasts

*The budget is based on the company's actual figures.* The idea is not to produce a budget based on vaguely estimated figures, but to work with data that has been carefully calculated and rigorously checked.

A budget is only of value if the forecasts it displays are in line with the reality it is supposed to describe.

2.  Active realism

*The budget is the roadmap to follow throughout the financial year.* It reflects the financial health of the company.

D.  Principle of affinity

Budget affinity is the expression of the functional conformity of the elements of the budget: the product, the activity and the consumer.

1.  Predictive affinity

*A good budget must anticipate changes in product costs.* It is essential to identify the key variables that influence revenue trends.

A newly-established company needs to gather information about seasonal fluctuations in its sector or its competitors' budgets.

2.  Active affinity

*Any amounts received or spent in relation to the budget forecasts must be recorded and accounted for.*

The principles of realism and appropriateness only apply to the first two phases of the budget: preparation and execution.

# Chapter II

**BUDGETARY INCOME**

## 11.1 What is a budget product?

Budgetary income refers to goods, services, levies, contributions and subsidies that are estimated in monetary terms and constitute the source of a company's revenue.

The sale of goods, the provision of services, levies, subsidies (and various forms of aid) and membership fees (for associations) are all sources of revenue for companies.

## 11.2 Characteristics of budgetary products

In practice, each budget product has two identifiers: its name and its intrinsic value.

## 11.3 Types of budgetary products

Budget products can be grouped into three categories:

1. Concrete products ;
2. Semi-concrete products ;
3. Abstract products.

Concrete products are those that are palpable. All the goods in a supermarket are tangible products.

Semi-concrete products are those that are not tangible, but can be represented by an image or material object. A mobile phone company sells services to the public, while the latter buys top-up cards, which are not, but do represent the company's products.

Abstract products are those which are not tangible, and which cannot be represented either by an image or by a material object. Taxes due to the public treasury are abstract products.

## 11.4 Consumers of budget products

Consumers are the persons (natural or legal) who are interested in the budgetary products of a given company and whose payment of a price enables the revenue provided for in the budget to be realised.

If the goods in a shop are the budgetary products of that shop, the buyers are the consumers. Similarly, school fees are the products of a school, but the pupils are the consumers.

To consume a budget item is to use it in return for payment of a consideration commensurate with its monetary value. Thus, a budget item used without payment of the consideration is considered as not consumed.

Goods in a shop are considered to have been consumed when the customer who used them has paid the consideration, otherwise the product is not consumed. Therefore, a pupil who has studied without paying has not consumed the school fees budget item.

N.B.

■ A budget item is overconsumed when its monetary value is lower than that of the counterparty.

■ A budget product is underconsumed when its monetary value is greater than that of the counterparty.

When the consumer uses the budgeted product by paying only part of its monetary value, there is partial consumption, because consumption is considered total if and only if the payment for the value of the product had been made in full. It is in this sense that the free use of a product by a consumer is considered non-consumption.

It should be noted, however, that when consumers are categorised and for the same product some consumers pay the total, others pay only part and a third category do not pay, consumption is always total when the consumer pays according to his category. Consumption is therefore considered total:

1. For a consumer in the first category who pays the full value of the product ;

2. For a consumer in the second category who pays part of the total value but corresponds to his category;

3. For a third category consumer who consumes the product free of charge.

Example

A health centre sets the rate for patients' medical consultations at an amount to be paid as follows:

- Ordinary patients pay in full;

- Conventional patients pay only half the rate;

- Consultation is free of charge for right holders.

| Consumer | Payment | | |
|---|---|---|---|
| | total | Half | Nothing |
| Rightful claimant | Overconsumption | Overconsumption | Normal consumption |
| Convention | Overconsumption | Normal consumption | No consumption |
| Ordinary patient | Normal consumption | Under consumption | No consumption |

## II.5 Types of budget revenue

Budgetary products can be :

- **Levies** whose calculation bases are not clearly defined, nor are they yet to be defined.

Levies are specific products of public services. Consumers of direct debits fall into two categories: those who can be listed and those who cannot.

Examples:

- IPR, Vignette whose consumers can be listed.
- Building permits, slaughtering costs for which consumers cannot be identified.
- **Similar to levies** are the budgetary products of companies which, in order to generate their revenues, offer the services they organise to consumers. These consumers, like those of levies, may or may not offer the possibility of establishing directories for their management.

Examples:

- Academic fees, subscriptions for which consumers can be identified.
- Medical consultation, travel ticket whose consumers cannot be identified.

- **Bills of exchange** are goods that are sold to consumers once they have been acquired without having been processed in any way.

Bills of exchange are the products of general trading companies, which buy goods for resale without further processing.

Examples:

- The different types of goods sold in a supermarket.
- Medicines sold in a pharmacy.

- **Processing effects** are the results of the transformation of raw materials by processing companies that buy the raw materials but sell the finished products obtained after transformation.

Examples:

- Bread sold in a bakery.
- Soaps in a soap factory.

- **Extraction effects** are the results of taking samples from nature.

All companies whose products come from nature are included in a category that includes activities such as :

- Fishing;
- Breeding ;
- Agriculture ;
- Planting ;
- Mining;
- Quarrying of construction materials ;
- Wood ;
- And so on.

The special feature of products in this category is that they are not purchased or processed, but come directly from nature.

Examples:

- The fish that make up the products of the fishery;
- Building stones from a quarrying company.

## II.6 Types of budget revenue

Budgetary income can be broken down into 5 different categories:

1. Random products;
2. Linear products ;
3. Rational products ;
4. Analytical products ;
5. Agricultural products.

A random product is a sample or sample-like product whose consumers are not known in advance and therefore do not offer the possibility of establishing directories.

Planning permission, for example, is a budget product. It is impossible to draw up a list of applicants for building permits when preparing the budget, as they are only known at the time of application.

The possibility or impossibility of drawing up lists of consumers is the point of difference between random and rational products, in that where it is possible to draw up lists of consumers, the products are said to be rational. Rational products are therefore levies or levy-like products whose consumers are known, and can be listed and therefore managed.

All goods are linear budget products because they are not processed before being put on sale.

Finished products belong to the analytical species because they result from the transformation of raw materials.

Agricultural products are the result of direct exploitation of the elements of nature.

| N° | Nature | Features | Species | Code |
|---|---|---|---|---|
| 1 | Levy or similar | No list of consumers | Aleatory | Al |
| 2 | Levy or similar | List of consumers | Rational | Ra |
| 3 | Buying effect | No transformation | Linear | Li |
| 4 | Transformation effect | Transformation of materials | Analytical | An |
| 5 | Extraction effect | Direct use of nature | Agricultural | Ag |

The same budget product can be both random and rational, but in its operation it remains either random or rational. In an insurance company, for example, the budget can be based on customer lists, or on seasonal fluctuations.

## II.7 Budget wastage

A. Notions

Budget wastage is defined as the loss, reduction or depreciation of the products or consumers involved in the preparation of budget forecasts.

Budget wastage occurs when the quantity of a budgeted product sold is less than the quantity forecast and when revenue is not achieved to the expected level. Therefore, budget wastage cannot be said to occur when the quantity of a budgeted product sold is greater than or equal to the quantity forecast, or when the revenue generated is greater than or equal to the forecast revenue.

Budget wastage manifests itself differently depending on the nature of the budget product under consideration: the sale of budget products is the main manifestation of goods, services assimilated to goods and finished products, whereas the budget wastage of levies and services assimilated to levies generally manifests itself through the insolvency of consumers.

B.  Loss factors

1.  Concept

Spoilage factors are the conditions that lead to the budgetary spoilage of a product by projecting the non-realisation of forecast revenues, thus creating a negative gap between the actual and forecast figures for the product concerned.

Wasting factors are generally social facts or natural phenomena. However, a social fact or a natural phenomenon that can be avoided cannot be considered as a factor of budget loss.

For example, a bread seller should avoid spreading his products evenly on the ground, rather than considering the humidity of the ground as a factor of budget loss.

The operator of a plant that converts raw materials into finished products needs to put in place security and surveillance measures, rather than seeing theft by its employees as a cost factor.

Anything that can be avoided cannot be considered as a budget wasting factor, otherwise it is a misjudgement that hampers the smooth running of the budget.

In a trading company, the two main causes of budget loss are, on the one hand, setting the price of budget products too low or too high and, on the other hand, the loss of goods, whereas in a school, insolvency is the manifestation of budgetary loss and the departure of pupils and the setting of a rate that is too low or too high are the two main factors in the loss of its products, i.e. school fees and other training-related costs.

2.  Influence of loss factors

Wasting factors are the conditions that favour budget wastage, and they generally influence consumers in the case of levies and levy-like services. A consumer affected by a wastage factor either does not consume the budgeted products or consumes without consideration, which prevents the company from realising the expected revenues.

Wastage factors generally affect budget products in the case of purchase effects, transformation effects and extraction effects. A budgetary product affected by a wastage factor prevents its consumption or causes under-consumption, which prevents the company from realising the expected revenues.

C.  Budget wastage rate

The wastage factors need to be identified and quantified in order to determine the budget wastage rate, i.e. the ratio between the value of the wastage and the total value, values relating to the quantity of budget products or consumers, but also the ratio between the amount of wastage and the total amount. It is this wastage rate that enables us to eliminate the deficit in advance so as to achieve a possible budget surplus at the end of the financial year.

The attrition rate (5) is then the ratio between the amount of attrition (D) and the total amount (T) of budget products; it is also the ratio between the number of attrition (D) and the total number (T) of consumers or budget products.

The number of budgetary products or consumers involved in the budgetary loss is referred to as the number of budgetary products or consumers involved in the budgetary loss, whereas the amount of loss is the amount not collected as a result of the influence of the budgetary loss.

$$\delta = \frac{D}{T} \times 100$$

5 : Budget wastage rate

D: Budget loss value (Loss headcount or Loss amount) T: Total value (Total headcount or Total amount)

Walk

$1^{cre}$ step: Identification of loss factors in relation to the products covered by the budget

$2^{c\,me}$ etape : Determination of the wastage value, i.e. the amount represented by the products affected by the wastage factors, the amount not collected or the actual wastage for each budget wastage factor.

Unpaid amount = Planned amount - Paid amount

Effective wastage = Amount not collected / Rate

$3^{c\,me}$ etape : Determination of the rate of budget wastage using the formula whereby the rate of budget wastage is the ratio between the value of the wastage and the total value of the products (or consumers) concerned in the budget.

$$\delta = \frac{D}{T} \times 100$$

## 11.8  Company categorisation

The Dewaz Method draws up the budget on the basis of additional tables, the number of which depends on the type of business in which the company operates.

Also, for pragmatic use, the Dewaz Method divides companies into three categories, in accordance with Article 3 of the OHADA Uniform Act on General Commercial Law and Articles 11 and 13 of the OHADA Uniform Act on the Organisation and Harmonisation of Company Accounts, namely :

o  Trading companies;

o  Industrial and craft businesses ;

o  Service companies ($1^{er}$ format and $2^{c}$ $^{me}$ format).

Service companies are divided into two categories, which suggests that the Dewaz Method presents four categories of company: trading companies, industrial companies, $1^{er}$ format service companies and $2^{c}$ $^{me}$ format service companies.

## 11.9  Budget type

The classification criteria used are product species and company sector of activity.

■  The budget of the rational type is appropriate for $1^{er}$ format service companies, those that use rational products.

The budgetary products of $1^{er}$ format service companies are levies or levy-like services that enable consumer lists to be drawn up.

Examples: Public services, education, insurance

The word rational is taken in the sense of the theory of mathematical logic, insofar as the consumers are known, it is possible to establish a direct link between the consumers and the products without going through intermediary calculations.

■  The appropriate random budget for $2^{eme}$ format service companies, those exploiting random products.

The budgetary products of service companies in $2^{eme}$ format are levies or levy-like services that do not offer the possibility of drawing up consumer lists.

Examples: Medical centre, Transport, Consultancy

The word "random" is used in the sense of probability theory. More specifically, the present value of future profits generated by a decision is a random variable whose probability distribution is assumed to be known.[9]

■  The appropriate linear budget for trading companies

The budget products of trading companies are goods that are bought for resale without being processed in any way.

---

[9] L. LESOURNE, Technique economique et gestion industrielle, Paris, 1971, p 36

Examples: Shop, pharmacy, Super Marche

The word linear is taken in the sense of theories of analytical geometry in the sense of variations that can be represented by a straight line, because it is the idea that products are sold as they are bought.

Everything you buy in trade has to be sold sooner or later.[10] Trading companies are those that buy goods in order to resell them without processing them in any way.

■ The appropriate analytical type of budget for industrial and craft companies

The budgetary products of industrial companies are the finished products produced after the transformation of raw materials.

Examples: Bakery, soap factory, creamery

The word "analytical" is understood to mean the complex calculations required to specify the finished products from the raw materials, through a series of transformations, and to determine their estimated value.

■ The budget for the agricultural type is appropriate for agricultural businesses, i.e. those that exploit nature.

The budgetary products of agricultural enterprises are the extraction effects coming directly from nature.

Examples: Planting, breeding, mining

Agriculture is understood to mean the direct exploitation of the elements of nature.

| N° | Sector of activity | Type of budget |
|---|---|---|
| 1 | Agriculture | Agricultural |
| 2 | Insurance | Aleatory or rational |
| 3 | General trade | Linear |
| 4 | Construction | Analytical |
| 5 | Education | Rational |
| 6 | Fishing | Agricultural |
| 7 | Manufacturing production | Analytical |
| 8 | Health | Aleatory |
| 9 | Public services | Aleatory or rational |
| 10 | Mobile telephony | Aleatory |
| 11 | Tourism | Aleatory |
| 12 | Transport | Aleatory |

---

[10] D. GRUNEWALD, Small BusinessManagement, New York, 1966, p 31

# Chapter III

## BUDGETARY ACTIVITIES

### 111.1 What is a budget activity?

The budget activities design the different areas of expenditure provided for in the budget with a view to avoiding haphazard allocations.

The revenue generated by the sale of budgetary products is intended to cover expenditure as specified in the budget in relation to the operation of budgetary activities, which are the statement of receipts and disbursements of a structure's funds.

Managing means forecasting, and forecasting means anticipating and preparing for the future.[11] This forecasting concerns not only budgetary income, but also budgetary activities with a view to making budgetary allocations possible.

### 111.2 Budgeting activities

In its operation, a budget activity may undergo entries, exits and processing. Each budget activity is housed in a budget item defined as a space reserved to contain the amount relating to a budget activity and to allow processing.

Drawing up a budget means forecasting both income and expenditure. It therefore means forecasting budgetary income, which is the source of the company's revenue, and budgetary activities, which are the areas in which expenditure is directed.

### 111.3 Budgetary framework

Strategic processes and tools (plans and budgets) offer a complementary way of understanding finance. The financial plan is a guide for the company; it enables the resources allocated to strategic actions to be divided between the various activities; the strategic budget is a quantified version of the financial plan.[12]

This is to say that, as the guide is important for the company's budget management, a repository is proposed as a company guide in order to be able to plan allocations in advance, as the different activities are represented by budget items where you just need to allocate a percentage to each activity to activate the process of allocating resources to the different activities.

The budget reference framework is a system for presenting the activities likely to be used for budget allocations in a given sector of activity. Budget items may be presented as a whole (the cartouche) or in detail (the outline).

---

[11] H. Fayol, L'administration industrielle et generale, Paris, 1979, p 35

[12] G. CAUSSE, Management financier, Sirey, 1979, p 149

## A.  The budget cartridge

The budget cartridge is a system of global presentation of all the items likely to be used for budget management in a specific sector of activity.

| BUDGET CARTRIDGE company directory | | | |
|---|---|---|---|
| **GROUP 1** | **GROUP 2** | **GROUP 3** | **GROUP 4** |
| Operating budget | Equipment budget | Intervention budget | Investment budget |
| 1. Staff remuneration | 5. Consumables | 8. Parallel activities | 11. Amortisation |
| 2. Owner puncture | 6. Maintenance and repair | 9. Social Assistance | 12. Placement |
| 3. Transfers | 7. Shareholdings | 10. Unforeseen | |
| 4. Operating expenses | | | |

Group 1 items record transactions that involve distributing the company's income between the owner, staff and those responsible for day-to-day management. Group 2 items record transactions relating to provisions and work to be carried out.

Group 3 items record transactions relating to activities that are not part of the company's regular operations.

Group 4 items record reserve transactions for subsequent use.

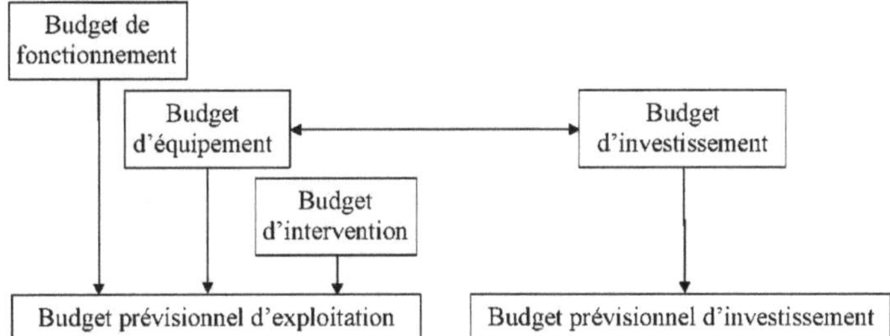


## B.  The budget outline

The budget outline is a detailed presentation of all the items likely to be used in a company's budget management.

The budget outline is distinguished according to whether it concerns one area of activity or another. In practice, for example, there is a trading budget outline, an industrial budget outline and so on.

While the budget cartridge is a global system, the outline is a detailed system for presenting all the budget items for a sector of activity.

<table>
<thead>
<tr><th colspan="5">COMPANY BUDGET OUTLINE</th></tr>
<tr><th colspan="3">GROUPES</th><th colspan="2">POSTS</th></tr>
<tr><th>N°</th><th>Designation</th><th>Securities</th><th>N°</th><th>Headings</th></tr>
</thead>
<tbody>
<tr><td rowspan="12">1</td><td rowspan="12">Budget Operating expenses</td><td rowspan="2">Staff remuneration</td><td>1.1</td><td>Employees</td></tr>
<tr><td>1.2</td><td>Active partners</td></tr>
<tr><td rowspan="3">Owner puncture</td><td>2.1</td><td>Owner's indemnities</td></tr>
<tr><td>2.2</td><td>Community holding</td></tr>
<tr><td>2.3</td><td>State levy</td></tr>
<tr><td rowspan="5">Operating costs</td><td>3.1</td><td>Administrative office</td></tr>
<tr><td>3.2</td><td>Technical office</td></tr>
<tr><td>3.3</td><td>Partner</td></tr>
<tr><td>3.4</td><td>Telephones</td></tr>
<tr><td>3.5</td><td>Fees and snacks</td></tr>
<tr><td rowspan="2">Disposals</td><td>4.1</td><td>Commissions</td></tr>
<tr><td>4.2</td><td>Rent and service charges</td></tr>
<tr><td rowspan="11">2</td><td rowspan="11">Equipment budget</td><td rowspan="5">Consumables</td><td>5.1</td><td>Administration supplies</td></tr>
<tr><td>5.2</td><td>Technical equipment</td></tr>
<tr><td>5.3</td><td>Maintenance supplies</td></tr>
<tr><td>5.4</td><td>Water and electricity</td></tr>
<tr><td>5.5</td><td>Other consumables</td></tr>
<tr><td rowspan="4">Maintenance and repair</td><td>6.1</td><td>Maintenance of premises</td></tr>
<tr><td>6.2</td><td>Furniture maintenance</td></tr>
<tr><td>6.3</td><td>Office equipment</td></tr>
<tr><td>6.4</td><td>Technical equipment</td></tr>
<tr><td rowspan="2">Shareholdings</td><td>7.1</td><td>Taxes</td></tr>
<tr><td>7.2</td><td>Insurance</td></tr>
<tr><td rowspan="3">3</td><td rowspan="3">Intervention budget</td><td>Parallel activities</td><td>8.1</td><td>Parallel activities</td></tr>
<tr><td>Social assistance</td><td>9.1</td><td>Social assistance</td></tr>
<tr><td>Unforeseen</td><td>10.1</td><td>Unforeseen</td></tr>
<tr><td rowspan="4">4</td><td rowspan="4">Investment budget</td><td rowspan="4">Amortization</td><td>11.1</td><td>Building</td></tr>
<tr><td>11.2</td><td>Furniture</td></tr>
<tr><td>11.3</td><td>Office equipment</td></tr>
<tr><td>11.4</td><td>Technical equipment</td></tr>
</tbody>
</table>

| | | Placement | 12.1 | Investment |
|---|---|---|---|---|
| | | | 12.2 | Reserve suppletive |

# Chapter IV

## THE ESTIMATED AMOUNT

To manage is to forecast, and to forecast is to anticipate and prepare for the future.[13] As we do not know the future with any certainty, we work with discounted income and try to get an idea of the influence that forecasting errors would have on discounted income. This leads us directly to a study of the risks of failing to realise expected income, which includes not only the theory of budget loss, but also that of the forecast amount (P).

The forecast amount is the present value of a company's future profits. According to Lessourne, if information is perfect, the decision will be the one that maximises the current value of the company.[14]

### 111.4 Budget staffing

The headcount is a central element in determining the forecast amount, however, the gross headcount is at the root of forecasting errors. Establishing the difference between the total headcount (T), the attrition headcount (D) and the actual headcount (K) is the first step towards solving the problem. Namely: the total workforce is taken without taking into account budget wastage; the wastage workforce concerns the products or consumers affected by budget wastage; the actual workforce is the difference between the first two.

### Total workforce (T)

The total number of employees is the number of consumers or budget products included in the budget.

### Wastage (D)

The attrition rate indicates the number of consumers or budget products affected by the attrition factors.

$$D = \frac{T \times \delta}{100}$$

### Actual workforce (K)

The actual headcount is the one to be taken into account when drawing up the budget. It represents the difference between the total headcount and the attrition headcount.

$$K = T - D$$

### IV.2 Budget consumption indicators

Consumption indicators are the elements used to determine the forecast amount of a budgeted product. The actual headcount, the rate and the gross margin are

---

[13] H. Fayol, L'administration industrielle et generale, Paris, 1979, p 35
[14] L. LESOURNE, Technique economique et Gestion industrielle, Paris, 1971, p 35

the consumption indicators used in the Dewaz method. **Forecast amount (P)**

The provisional amount is the projected sum to be realised on a given budget product.

$$P = K \times vi$$

For rational and random types

$$P = K \times MB$$

For linear and analytical types

**IV.3 Budget consumption parameters**

Consumption parameters are the elements used to determine the forecast headcount (T) of a budget product when drawing up the budget. The consumption cycle (C), the consumption frequency (F) and the consumption coefficient$^{(\lambda)}$ are the three consumption parameters used in the Dewaz Method. It should be noted that the budget of the rational type does not use the consumption parameters to determine the forecast headcount, because, being the only type which uses consumer directories which are known in advance, the forecast headcount is not calculated, because the different directories and the consumer headcount determine it from the outset.

**Consumption cycle (C)**

1. Definition

The consumption cycle of a product is a regular period in which a sequence of consumption of this product takes place in a given order.

2. Expression

A product's consumption cycle can be hourly, daily, weekly, monthly, quarterly, annual, etc. The sales cycle of a product is not calculated, it is observed.

**Consumption coefficient** $^{(\lambda)}$

1. Definition

The consumption coefficient of a product indicates the number of consumption cycles of this product contained in a budget year.

2. Expression

Exercise

$$\lambda = \frac{Exercice}{C}$$

Here, the exercise and the consumption cycle must be expressed in the same unit of measurement, i.e. day, week, month, etc.

**Consumption frequency (F)**

1. Definition

The rate at which a product flows through its consumption cycle is known as its consumption frequency.

So the frequency of a product can be daily, weekly, monthly, quarterly, annually, etc.

2. Expression

The frequency of consumption is expressed by the number of occurrences in relation to the periodicity expressed in the consumption cycle.

$$F = n / p$$

n = Number of occurrences

p = Periodicity expressed in the consumption cycle

Example: 7/day, 2/week, 10/month

The consumption parameters are not linked to the budget year, but to a budget product for the year.

**Total workforce (T)**

1. Notion

Total headcount indicates the number of times a product occurs in a financial year.

2. Formula

$$T = F \times \lambda$$

Use not valid for the budget of the rational type.

**IV.4 Budget potential**

Budgetary potential refers to the total capacity of a budget. It is the present value of a company's future profits without taking depletion into account.

It should be noted that the potential amount depends on the budget year, because each budget product gives its potential $(\pi_i)$, and the total of all the potentials of the budget products constitutes the potential $(\pi)$ of the budget.

**A. The potential of products $(\pi_i)$**

Each budget product gives rise to a corresponding potential $\pi_i$. Thus, as many budgetary products, as many potential amounts $\pi_i$ different from the potential $\pi$ corresponding to the sum of all the potentials $\pi_i$.

Each budget product has a potential amount, which is the product of its rate or gross margin and the total number of products or consumers concerned in the budget.

For rational and random products

$$\pi_i = T \times vi$$

For linear and analytical products

$$\pi_i = T \times MB$$

## B. Budget potential ( )$^\pi$

The potential amount ($\pi$ ) is the sum determined as a function of the total capacity of the budget. It is the sum of the potential amounts of the various products concerned in the budget.

$$\pi = \pi_1 + \pi_2 + \pi_3 + \dots \pi_n$$

The budget potential is different from the forecast in that the potential does not take into account the budget loss, whereas the forecast is calculated without the budget loss.

The budget estimate (P) is a budget amount that is calculated without budgetary deductions. It is therefore the amount to be considered when drawing up the budget.

The budgetary potential (л) is an amount used in the budget as an indication in order to determine the amount and rate of wastage in both the drafting and control of the budget.

It should also be noted that a company's budget potential represents its total capacity, whereas a company's budget forecast represents its achievable potential.

So drawing up a company's budget on the basis of its potential can only lead to budgetary aberration.

## IV.5 Budget implementation rate

The ratio between the budget forecast and the budget realised is known as the budget realisation rate. The overall amount of the forecast is that of the centraliser, the amount of the realisation is that of the capitalist.

$$\rho = \frac{R}{P} \times 100$$

p: Budget implementation rate

P : Planned amount

R: Real amount

This rate indicates the extent to which the budget has been achieved.

If p > 100%, the budget is in surplus.

If p < 100%, the budget is in deficit.

If p = 100%, the budget is balanced.

And the difference constitutes the budget balance, surplus or deficit.

The realisation rate can be calculated by product, by area or by category.

# Chapter V

# THE AGRICULTURAL BUDGET

## V.1 Concepts

The budgetary management of companies whose budgetary income comes from the exploitation of nature highlights an exception to be studied in particular. In this category of activities, we find :

- Fishing;
- Breeding ;
- Agriculture ;
- Planting ;
- Mining;
- Quarrying of construction materials ;
- Wood ;
- And so on.

All these activities have one thing in common: their budgetary products are found directly in nature, and production is natural in the sense that human intervention is only felt on the input side for preparation and on the output side for exploitation, but production is natural.

By their very nature, all agricultural products are extracts. But in the course of production, an extraction product may or may not be transformed for consumption. This is why there is no such thing as a pure agricultural product, and why the consumption of agricultural products depends on the trend.

A distinction is made between :

- Agricultural products with a random trend;
- Agricultural products with a linear trend;
- Rational agricultural products;
- Agricultural products have an analytical tendency.

## V.2 Nature and species

Agricultural budget products are all of the same nature and type. They are products of extraction belonging to the category of agricultural products.

| Sector | Budgetary income |
|---|---|
| Water | Water |
| Fishing | Fish and other aquatic products |
| Hunting | Animals and animal products: meat, skin, blood, milk, excrement, etc. |
| Harvesting | Plants, fruit, leaves, bark, roots, seeds, branches, etc. |
| Breeding | Animals and animal products: meat, skin, |

| | blood, milk, excrement, etc. |
|---|---|
| Agriculture | Plants, fruit, leaves, bark, roots, seeds, branches, etc. |
| Planting | Plants, fruit, leaves, bark, roots, seeds, branches, etc. |
| Mining | Precious stones |
| Quarrying of construction materials | Sand, building stone and other materials |
| The wood | Logs, wood |

**V.3 Permanent and renewable products**

In their exploitation, agricultural products are permanent or renewable depending on whether they offer the possibility of exploitation in a continuous or discontinuous rhythm according to their permanent or alternative presence.

Permanent products are those for which nature offers the possibility of being exploited on a permanent basis. They are products that can be found without interruption in time and space.

The following sectors are considered as permanent products:
- Fishing;
- Mini-holding;
- Quarrying of construction materials ;
- Wood ;
- And so on.

Renewable products are those that are harvested over specific periods.

These are products from the :
- Planting ;
- Breeding ;
- Agriculture ;
- And so on.

It should be noted that a permanent product may be renewable for a period of time. Fishing may be suspended for a specific period in order to renew the quantity of fish in the waters. Hunting may also take place under the same conditions. In these cases, the products of fishing and hunting are not permanent but renewable, whereas they are naturally permanent.

**V.4 Budget scale**

**A. What is a budget scale?**

The budget scale designates the element of nature that needs to be exploited to produce agricultural budget products. The budget scale can be water, a plot of land, a quarry, a beast, a tree, a plant, a field, a bush, and so on.

**B. Features**

A budget scale is characterised by the quantity and quality of its budgetary products and its capacity in relation to each of its budgetary products.

Budget products in the scale

| Scale | Budgetary income |
|---|---|
| Water | Fish and other aquatic products |
| Carriere | Precious stones, building stones, sand, etc. |
| Field | Plants, vegetables, fruit, leaves, roots, etc. |
| Bete | Small animals, meat, skin, eggs, milk, hair, excrement, etc. |
| Tree | Fruit, leaves, bark, roots, seeds, branches, etc. |

## C. The capacity of a ladder

The capacity of a scale indicates the quantity of products it contains in relation to a given budget year. A distinction is made between static capacity ($k_s$) linked to the scale itself and dynamic capacity ($k_d$) linked to the budgetary products of the budgetary scale.

The static capacity of a scale in relation to a budgeted product is the quantity of this product contained in the scale in accordance with the budget year.

Static capacity is expressed by the quantity of products it contains. A tree bearing 2,000 fruits has a static capacity of 2,000 fruits.

The dynamic capacity of a scale, in relation to a budget product, indicates the quantity that it can be used for during the financial year.

It should be pointed out that the quantity to be harvested depends on the time required, the number of people involved and the quality and quantity of the equipment used.

The dynamic capacity of a scale in relation to a product is expressed by the quantity it is capable of producing over a period to be coupled with the operating parameters, i.e. man, time and material.

## D. Operating parameters

These are the resources that combine to determine the forecast quantity of agricultural budget products. Three elements make up the operating parameters, namely :

- The man,
- Time, - Equipment.

How many people are needed at what time to use what equipment to produce what quantity of budget products?

It should be pointed out that operating parameters are not calculated, they are observed in practice. There is no formula that can be used to determine the values of the operating parameters, as detailed observation is sufficient to determine the operating parameters of an agricultural product in relation to a given scale.

<u>The man</u>

The number of people required to operate a ladder in order to produce a certain quantity of product.

<u>The material</u>

The material to be used is more than fundamental to the production of budget products. You always have to ask yourself what equipment you need to produce the best results. And in what quantities?

<u>The weather</u>

The use of a scale for production lasts over time. If the scale is the space in which the operation takes place, we also need to know how long it takes to produce a certain quantity of budget products.

## V.5 The production determinant

The determinant is a table that combines the various production parameters of a budgeted product to determine its forecast quantity, known as dynamic capacity (Kd).

Production is the fundamental element of the agricultural budget. The budgetary products that need to be consumed to generate revenue are not manufactured or purchased, but obtained by exploiting nature.

In farming, everything we sell is the result of exploiting nature. For this reason, the elements of the determinant must include the parameters of exploitation in order to achieve dynamic capacity.

Scale :

| N° | Product | | Ks | Parameters | | | Kd |
|---|---|---|---|---|---|---|---|
| | Designation | Code | | m | t | h | |
| | | | | | | | |
| | | | | | | | |

Keeping the production determinant enables us to determine the exact quantity to be produced, so as to avoid proposing an over- or under-quantity in the sales forecasts for budgeted products.

## Scale

The scale designates the element of nature that must be exploited in order to obtain agricultural produce. The budgetary scale can be water, land, a quarry, a beast, a tree, a plant, a field, a bush, etc.

## Static capacity (Ks)

The static capacity (Ks) of a scale in relation to a given agricultural budget product is the quantity of this product contained in the scale concerned. Static capacity may also be indeterminate.

**Variable h**

1. Notion

The variable h represents the number of men required to operate the scale over time using appropriate equipment in order to produce a given quantity of a budgeted product from the scale.

2. Expression

The variable h is expressed as a pair ($h_{min}$, $h_{max}$ ). The minimum workforce $h_{min}$ is the number of men required to use the equipment to produce the minimum quantity of budget product. The maximum workforce $h_{max}$ is the largest number of people required to produce a budgeted quantity of a scale.

**Variable t**

1. Notion

The variable t represents the time required to operate a ladder in order to produce a certain quantity of budget product. The different values of the variable t vary from the minimum to the maximum, passing through intermediate values.

2. Expression

The variable t is expressed as a pair ($t_{min}$ , $t_{max}$ ). The minimum time $t_{min}$ is the time it takes to use the equipment to produce the minimum budgeted output. It is the time that can never be exceeded without achieving a certain output. The minimum time is generally expressed in hours, but it can also be expressed in other units. The maximum duration $t_{max}$ is the number of $t_{min}$ contained in a budget year.

$t_{max} = n \cdot t_{min}$

n is the number of months in the budget year.

n is to be determined on the basis of the calendar, spreading the various $t_{min}s$ over the working hours contained in the exercise.

**Variable m**

1. Notion

The variable m represents the material required to operate a ladder in order to produce a certain quantity of budget product.

2. Expression

The variable m is expressed as a triplet ($m_i$, $m_2$, $m_3$). $m_i$ represents the quality of the material, and $m_2$ is the quantity needed to use the ladder for production. $m_3$ represents the way the material is used; its value is i when used individually and c when used collectively.

Examples

i. (Pirogue, i, c)

2 (Knife, 2, i)

**Dynamic capacity (Kd)**

The dynamic capacity (Kd) of a scale in relation to a given agricultural budget product is the quantity of this product which the scale offers the possibility of exploiting according to the production parameters, namely: human resources, the time it takes and the equipment to be used.

The dynamic capacity (Kd) of a scale in relation to a given agricultural budget product is a function of the variables h and t in their evolution for the exploitation of the budget product concerned.

To determine the dynamic capacity, simply combine the different values of the h variable with those of the t variable using the value chessboard.

**Stock chart**

| t | | Min | Max |
|---|---|---|---|
| h | | | |
| Min | | | |
| Max | | | |

The range of values is product by product, so each budget product has its own range of values.

The columns of the chessboard are filled with the values of the variable h, and the rows are filled with the values of the variable t, which can be determined by simple observation.

Dynamic capacity is obtained by combining the variables h and t, and occupies the square on the chessboard where the column meets the row.

Present the chessboard of values for the quarterly work of a fisherman who works 6 hours a day with a net to catch an average of 4 large fish and 25 small fish, knowing that he does not work on Saturdays and Sundays. $t_{min}$ = 6 hours n = 67 $h_{min}$ = 1

$t_{max}$ = 402 hours $\quad h_{max}$ = 1

Large poisons

| h | t | Min | Max |
|---|---|---|---|
| | | 6 hours | 402 hours |
| Min | 1 | 4 fish | 268 fish |
| Max | 1 | 4 fish | 268 fish |

Small fish

| h | t | Min | Max |
|---|---|---|---|
| | | 6 hours | 402 hours |
| Min | 1 | 25 fish | 1,675 fish |
| Max | 1 | 25 fish | 1,675 fish |

The determinant is a budget table that is not part of the budget plan, but a table that can be consulted to compare the quantity to be produced with the quantity to be sold, so as to ensure that the quantity to be produced is always greater than the quantity to be sold.

| |
| --- |
| If T < Kd, the budget is possible |
| If T > Kd, there is a budget impasse upstream |

# Chapter VI

# APPLICATIONS OF THE DEWAZ METHOD

## VI.1 Concepts

The implementation of all the theories developed in the Dewaz Method requires the presence of applications whose handling translates the materialization of the Dewaz Method in the functioning of companies. These applications, which are derivatives of the Dewaz Method, are :

1. Budgeting;
2. The budget procedure ;
3. The Integrated Budget System.

The Dewaz Method enables companies to be managed in 3 phases: budget preparation, execution and re-evaluation, all of which require an appropriate budgeting technique. In this sense, budgeting, an offshoot of the Dewaz Method, is a budgeting technique for drawing up, managing and evaluating company budgets.

In day-to-day management, the 3 phases of the Dewaz Method each contain a certain number of operations to be carried out, which together make up the budgetary procedure defined as the logical sequence of operations relating to the functioning of the company budget. It should be noted that each budgetary operation corresponds to a specific job. In addition to budgetary operations, the budgetary procedure therefore defines budgetary professions for the use of the Dewaz Method in corporate governance.

How can companies be monitored within a single system? The answer seems to be a three-component mechanism, with the Dewaz Method at its centre, with public and private companies on one side and public services on the other. This is the Integrated Budget System, derived from the Dewaz Method, in which the Dewaz Method is used by companies for good governance and by the public services to monitor and supervise companies, both public and private.

In practical terms, the budgetary applications of the Dewaz Method, i.e. budgeting, the budgetary procedure and the Integrated Budgeting System (IBS), are the various facets of the Dewaz Method without which it would remain pure theory and of little use in corporate governance. In other words, budget applications put the Dewaz Method into practice by enabling company budgets to function.

## VI.2 Budgeting

### A.  What is budgeting?

Budgeting is a technique for drawing up budget forecasts that can be used to manage the budget and, at the end of the financial year, to identify variances between actual and forecast budget.

The technique is carried out using complementary tables and in three phases:

> Budget preparation ;

> Budget management ;

> Budget assessment.

Budgeting exploits the successive properties of budget tables to help companies draw up, manage and re-evaluate their budgets.

## B. Budget type

Corporate budget management varies according to the type of budget product and the sector in which the company operates. A distinction is made between: aleatory budgeting, linear budgeting, rational budgeting, analytical budgeting and agricultural budgeting.

The classification criteria used are the type of budget product and the company's sector of activity.

| Budget type | Sector of activity | Budgetary income |
|---|---|---|
| Rational budgeting | Public services and service companies | Samples or similar with lists of consumers |
| Random budgeting | Public services and service companies | Sampling or similar without consumer lists |
| Linear budgeting | Trading companies | Purchase notes |
| Analytical budgeting | Industrial companies | Transformation effects |
| Agricultural budgeting | Budget scale operating companies | Extraction effects |

■ Rational budgeting for service companies (1$^{er}$ format) Education, insurance, associations, etc.

■ Random budgeting for service companies (2$^{eme}$ format) Medical centres, transport, consultancy firms, etc.

■ Linear budgeting for trading companies Boutique, pharmacy, Super Marche, etc.

■ Analytical budgeting for industrial and craft companies Bakeries, soap factories, creameries, etc.

■ Agricultural budgeting for industrial and craft businesses Fisheries, plantations, farms, etc.

| N° | Sector of activity | Type of budget |
|---|---|---|
| 1 | Education | Rational budgeting |
| 2 | Health | Random budgeting |
| 3 | General trade | Linear budgeting |
| 4 | Manufacturing production | Analytical budgeting |

| 5 | Mobile telephony | Random budgeting |
| 6 | Transport | Random budgeting |
| 7 | Construction | Analytical budgeting |
| 8 | Tourism | Random budgeting |
| 9 | Public services | Rational budgeting |
| 10 | Insurance | Rational budgeting |

### ■ I.3 The budget procedure

### A. What is the budget procedure?

The budgetary procedure refers to a logical sequence of operations relating to the functioning of the budget, from its conception to its evaluation.

The following are considered budgetary transactions :

1. Budget design ;
2. Drafting the budget ;
3. Budgeting ;
4. Budget management ;
5. Budget transcription ;
6. Budget monitoring ;
7. Budget audit ;
8. Budgetary control.

The budgetary procedure is clearly divided into three stages, which occur every time a company is faced with a decision. These are: forecasting, budgeting and control.[15]

Forecasting: preliminary study of the decision ;

Budgeting: defining objectives and resources ;

Control: obtaining variances between target and actual.

### B. Budget operations

### 1. Budget design

Budget design involves setting up a budget system to enable budget preparation operations to be carried out.

The budgeting system is based on the idea of providing operational staff with a number of useful tools for the management process.

Budget design involves studying the budget products and their environment to determine not only the type of budget but also the different budget tables to be used.

### 2. Drafting the budget

Drawing up a budget involves determining in advance the income and expenditure of a given structure by keeping tables for this purpose. These tables

---

[15] J. MEYER, Gestion budgetaire, Paris, 1979, p 22

serve as a compass for the rest of the budgetary operations.

## 3. Budgeting

Budgeting consists of inserting the revenue and expenditure provided for in the budget.

## 4. Budget management

Budget management consists of ensuring that revenue and expenditure are achieved in line with budget forecasts.

## 5. Budget transcription

Transcribing the budget involves recording and accounting for income and expenditure in accordance with budget forecasts in the tables provided for this purpose.

## 6. Budget monitoring

Budget monitoring consists of tracking budget income and expenditure on a day-to-day basis in order to identify any variances.

The main objective of budget monitoring is to find out whether the transcription is being carried out in accordance with the forecasts as drawn up and presented in the design tables.

## 7. Budget assessment

Budgetary evaluation consists of comparing the preparation of budgetary forecasts with their implementation in order to identify any variances.

Budget evaluation can be internal or external. It is internal when it is carried out by an in-house agent (Budget Auditor), whereas it is external when it is carried out by outside expertise.

External evaluation can be either legal or contractual. Legal evaluation, also known as budgetary control, is compulsory and is carried out by State agents (Budget Controllers) with a mandate issued by a competent authority.

The contractual evaluation, also known as an external budget audit, is carried out by a specialist company or by an independent agent (Budget Auditor) on behalf of the organisation.

Whether the evaluation is internal or external, legal or contractual, the approach is the same. The only difference is that the objectives are different depending on whether it is a budgetary audit or a budgetary control. Budgetary audit, whether internal or external, is always incentive-based, whereas budgetary control is punitive.

## C. Jobs related to the budgetary procedure

In the budget procedure, each of the operations is carried out by a clearly defined specialist.

| N° | Budget operations | Budget specialists |
|---|---|---|
| 1 | Budget design | The Budget Designer |

| 2 | Drafting the budget | The Budget Writer |
|---|---|---|
| 3 | Budgeting | The Budget Writer |
| 4 | Budget management | The Budget Driver |
| 5 | Budget transcription | The Budget Operator |
| 6 | Budget monitoring | The Budget Analyst |
| 7 | Budget audit | The Budget Auditor |
| 8 | Budgetary control | The Budget Controller |

## 1. The Budget Designer

The Budget Designer is a specialist who studies the company's environment and budget products to determine the type of budget and the tables to be used for drafting the budget.

## 2. The Budget Writer

The Budget Writer is a specialist who is responsible for maintaining the design tables to determine the company's income and expenditure in advance.

## 3. The Budget Driver

The Budget Manager is a specialist who ensures that income and expenditure are achieved in line with budget forecasts.

## 4. The Budget Operator

The Budget Operator is a specialist who is responsible for maintaining management tables for recording and accounting for income and expenditure in line with budget forecasts.

## 5. The Budget Analyst

The Budget Analyst is a specialist in the day-to-day monitoring of budget income and expenditure with a view to establishing any variances.

## 6. The Budget Auditor

The Budget Auditor is a specialist who is responsible for maintaining the mosaic tables by comparing actual and forecast budgets to identify variances.

The Budget Auditor is internal when he or she is a member of the company's staff, external when he or she is not.

## 7. The Budget Controller

The Budget Controller is a specialist who, under a legal mandate, is responsible for maintaining the mosaic tables by comparing actual and forecast budgets in order to identify variances.

The Internal Auditor, the External Auditor and the Budget Controller are all specialists whose job it is to re-evaluate the budget.

### VI.4 The Integrated Budget System (IBS)

### A. What is the Integrated Budgeting System?

The Integrated Budgeting System (IBS) is a management mechanism, the core of which is the Dewaz Method, which enables efficient management of public and private companies and effective monitoring and supervision of these companies by the relevant public services.

Systeme because it is a process with varied objects for overall operation; Budgetary because the process targets a specific area, the budget; Integrated because adaptation to the Dewaz Method is essential for companies and public services.

According to Lapierre, a system is made up of interdependent elements whose links are such that if one of them is modified, the others are also modified and, as a result, the whole is transformed.[16]

The components of the Integrated Budgetary System can function in isolation for other purposes, but in the organisation of the system, functioning in isolation is practically impossible because of their interdependence, since each of the elements always depends on two others for its proper, harmonious functioning.

The development of the standard of living, according to Taylor, and consequently the modification of the way of life which is made possible by the accumulation of material goods, derive essentially from the search for new means and from the organisation of human societies which apply these means.[17]

It is therefore important to specify that, in the conditions of this development, the Dewaz Method, which is part of the practical life of companies, is presented as a proposed guide for the management and control of companies.

## B. **Structure**

The Integrated Budgeting System is a machine with three complex parts:

1. The Dewaz Method in the centre;
2. Public and private companies at a crossroads;
3. Public services at the other end of the scale.


[16] J W. LAPIERRE, L'analyse des systemes politiques, Paris, 1973, p 67
[17] F.W. Taylor, La direction scientifique des entreprises, Paris, 1967, p 9

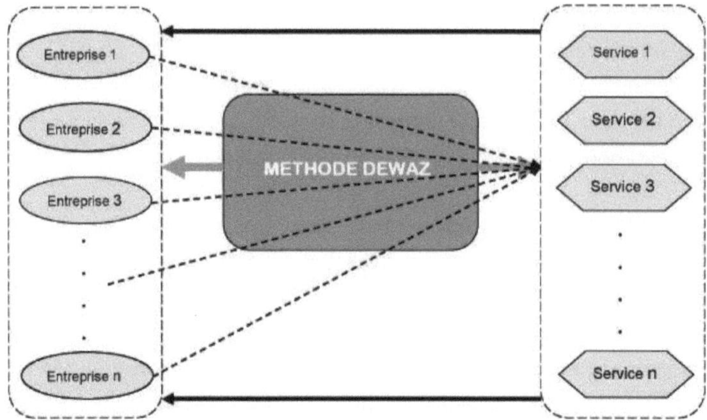


The method provides companies with 1 management tool

The method provides public services with 1 company monitoring tool
Public services provide a framework for businesses
► Companies pay taxes
Public services control companies

## C. **Features**

Used by companies, the Dewaz Method is a management tool for drawing up, executing and evaluating budgets using supplementary tables. Public services use the Dewaz Method as a control tool to monitor and supervise public and private companies.

BIBLIOGRAPHY

1. **Basle**, Maurice
Le Budget de 1 Etat, Paris, 1997
2. **CAUDE**, Roland
Comment prevoir, Paris, 1978
3. **CAUSSE**, Genevieve, Alain **CHEVALIER** and Georges **HIRSCH**
Management financier, Sirey, 1979
4. **CONSO,** Pierre
Dictionnaire de gestion financiere, Paris, 1979
5. **FAHEY**, L and R. RANDALL
Les parametres essentiels de la gestion strategique, Paris, 1997
6. **FAYOL**, Henry
Administration generale et industrielle, Paris, 1976
7. **GRUNEWALD**, Donald
Small Business Management, New York, 1966
8. **LAPIERRE**, J W
L'analyse des systemes politiques, Paris, 1973
9. **LESOURNE**, L
Technique economique et gestion industrielle, Paris, 1971
10. **LOEB**, Paul
Le budget de l'entreprise, Paris, 1956
11. **MEYER**, Jean
Gestion budgetaire, Paris, 1979
12. **SEKA SEKA** Paul
Public Finance Course, Abidjan, 2012
13. **TAYLOR** Winslow Frederic
La direction scientifique des entreprises, Paris, 1967

Buy your books fast and straightforward online - at one of world's fastest growing online book stores! Environmentally sound due to Print-on-Demand technologies.

Buy your books online at
**www.morebooks.shop**

Kaufen Sie Ihre Bücher schnell und unkompliziert online – auf einer der am schnellsten wachsenden Buchhandelsplattformen weltweit! Dank Print-On-Demand umwelt- und ressourcenschonend produziert.

Bücher schneller online kaufen
**www.morebooks.shop**

MIX
Papier aus verantwortungsvollen Quellen
Paper from responsible sources
FSC® C105338
FSC
www.fsc.org